TO: JAMES M
Thank you for your support.
I hope you enjoy my book.

Marlena Flowers
H

Renewing of your Mind & Spirit for Marriage

From single to married

Marlena Flowers

authorHOUSE

AuthorHouse™
1663 Liberty Drive
Bloomington, IN 47403
www.authorhouse.com
Phone: 1-800-839-8640

© 2011 Marlena Flowers. All rights reserved.

No part of this book may be reproduced, stored in a retrieval system, or transmitted by any means without the written permission of the author.

First published by AuthorHouse 5/17/2011

ISBN: 978-1-4389-4335-0 (sc)

Library of Congress Control Number: 2010910664

Printed in the United States of America

Any people depicted in stock imagery provided by Thinkstock are models, and such images are being used for illustrative purposes only. Certain stock imagery © Thinkstock.

This book is printed on acid-free paper.

Because of the dynamic nature of the Internet, any web addresses or links contained in this book may have changed since publication and may no longer be valid. The views expressed in this work are solely those of the author and do not necessarily reflect the views of the publisher, and the publisher hereby disclaims any responsibility for them.

Scriptures are taken from the King James Version Bible.
Copyright 1994© by The Zondervan Corporation

Fictitious names have been used throughout the book except in the dedication.

*D*edication

This book is lovingly dedicated to my daughter, Jazzmine Davis.

Acknowledgements

A special thank you to my Dad Charles Flowers, my sisters, brothers and all of my family and friends that have supported me and encouraged me through my journey of being taught how to be a wife and throughout my life.

I am truly grateful to Kevin & Ronee, Bridget, Linda, Charlecia, Beverly, Gayle, Charlene, Xavier, Rochelle, Darlene, Michelle and Keith. Thank you for all your support and work towards helping me publish.

Last but not least, I like to thank my friend, my comforter, my Lord & Savior. Thank you God for you grace and mercy and unfailing love.

Renewing of Your Mind & Spirit for Marriage

And be not conformed to this world; but be ye transformed by the renewing of your mind, that ye may prove what is that good, and acceptable, and perfect, will of God. Romans 12: 2

Table of Contents

The Beginnings	1
Mind & Spirit Being Renewed	3
Spirit of Desperation	5
Chaotic Relationship	11
Renewal to Get to My Promise	13
The Test	19
Off Path of My Promise	23
Pressing Through	29
What Is the Reason for the Relationship Anyway?	33
Pour Into Me	35
Looking Beyond the Situation to See God	39
Worship	43
The Quest for Submission	49
Testimonies of Married Men & Women	53
Arguments	67
Patience	73
Your Anointing	75
What Are You Going to Do Differently?	79

The Beginnings

I had a very good childhood—two-parent home, youngest of six—and I was spoiled beyond measure. We grew up in a neighborhood where we stayed out all night, played hide and seek and "catch a girl get a girl" (although we were really too young to do anything besides clothes burn). My father is a great Dad, and my Mom was a wonderful Mom and wife who cooked three-course meals every day except Saturdays, when she went to bingo.

I have a brother about three years older than me, so dating boys was out of the question. Plus, he was tough, and everybody knew that he would beat them down if they even thought about dating me. I was able to talk on the phone with boys in the eighth grade, which was cool, but I much preferred being outside playing double-dutch or making up dance routines with my girlfriends.

By the time I entered ninth grade, my brother let loose, and I was free to date—not that I was thinking about that, but it was now an option. I was mostly excited about high school and going from building to building to get to class. The first guy I dated was this a guy I had a crush on in junior high school. We began going out, and it was wonderful.

My parents allowed him to come over, and we just kicked it. One of my older sisters took us shopping and out to eat, she kept us busy.

Five years later, we were still dating and had a child together. We broke up about a year and a half later, because he had another baby with a girl whom he was dating on and off while he and I were together.

My desire is to share my journey of being single while learning what I needed in order to renew my mind and spirit for a healthy relationship and ultimately marriage. While on this journey I discovered that there is a difference in the mindset of married people and the mindset of single people as it relates to relationships and marriage. I discovered this when I was visiting a recently married girlfriend. She had a mixture of single and married women there discussing life in general and of course we began to talk about men and relationships. Some single women shared their dating experiences and most of us were saying that we hated dating and wanted to be married. The married women shared some of their experiences as wives. As I sat there listening, God began to reveal to me that there are very distinct differences between the mindset of single women and married women.

As the night progressed it was clear that God was revealing the need for single people to renew their minds and spirits before marriage.

Mind & Spirit Being Renewed

For as long as I can remember, I wanted to be married although, my Mother and Father never raised us to be wives but to be independent, in fact I am the only sibling that wanted to be married. At the age of twenty-nine, I was still unmarried, and there were no potentials in sight. In February 2005, I made my first visit to Life Church. During this visit, it was prophesied by Pastor Terry that God was going to teach me how to be a wife and that my husband would be in the ministry. I thought to myself, *what does that mean? Teach me how to be a wife?* I really didn't know what that meant but I knew anything that God had for me was good and especially if it had to do with me getting married, I was game! I was anxiously awaiting some big change to come over me from heaven. I knew that I was what some would call "really single". I would come home and go straight to sleep, coming and going as I pleased. (Single women know what I am talking about!) Weeks passed after this was spoken to me and I was still waiting for a big change in my life. In my mind, being a wife meant cooking, cleaning, raising children, and having a house on the hill, a boat on the lake, and a home with a white picket fence. To add to all of my original misconceptions, I also believed it meant always having a date and being able to have sex legally—that was it!

After about a month of expecting something to drop from heaven (which didn't happen), I began to pray and asked God what did he mean about teaching me how to be a wife? And when was He going to teach me because I was ready to get married. This was just the beginning of my journey on renewing my mind and spirit for marriage and it did not occur over night. I begin writing this book in March of 2006, and since then, there have been several instances of rejection, disappointment, failed relationships, and long periods of loneliness. I pray through reading about my journey you will be blessed by what God has taught me about being a wife and about relationships in general. I also hope that your journey to marriage or whatever it is you desire from God, will not take you as long to receive it as it has taken me, due to lack of knowledge. It is my sincere prayer that your mind and spirit will be renewed before marriage.

Spirit of Desperation

There is an evil spirit that goes completely unnoticed. It's the spirit of desperation! Desperation is reckless behavior out of fear, anxiety and hopelessness. It makes you fearful of never getting your heart's desires and leads to unhealthy compromise.

One example of unhealthy compromise is when one ignores signs of an unfaithful mate. One man can be dating five women at the same time, and they'll all think that he is their husband. How is that possible? Because the spirit of desperation in them has caused them to ignore the signs that he is seeing other people. As much as you want to have someone in your life, you cannot always have Mr. Right Now, because he could be blocking Mr. Forever. Men, will have three and four women at the same time because they are afraid to be alone. This may cause them to miss out on their wife. Ten years later, they could find themselves in the barbershop unmarried, lonely and miserable, talking about how they missed out on someone special!

The spirit of desperation makes you feel that you will always be alone. It makes you feel that because you are getting older it is too late in life for you to get married and have a family. It makes you feel as if God doesn't care about you getting married. The word of God teaches us that marriage is honorable. (Hebrews 13:4) Your spouse represents God's love for you in the flesh. Truly, marriage is a gift from God. Why then would God not be concerned?

I encourage you to go to God in prayer and be honest and say what's on your heart. My prayer has been the following: "Lord I want him to be with me; I want him to love me and to have a family, so if it's in your will let it be so as I desire and have asked. Let there be peace in our hearts and let us be one according to your will and plan for our lives." After praying about the relationship I try my best to leave it to God, for His will to be done and I allow God's peace to rest in my heart no matter the outcome.

There were times when I was not as confident in going to God about a relationship but wanted my will to be done. On numerous occasions, one of my girlfriends and I had conversations about how it's scary to ask God if the person you are dating is the one, because the answer might be no. What's important to keep in mind is that whatever God has planned for you is only what is good, perfect, and acceptable. If the person you are dating is good, perfect, and acceptable then there is no need to be afraid to pray and ask God the reason for the relationship. If you desire to be married and it's in God's will for you to be married, then you will get married. However, you must trust God and seek after His will for your life. Again, if it is in God's plan he will create an opportunity for you to meet your spouse and give you wisdom and help to have a successful relationship and marriage.

It is important to seek God **first** through prayer to know the purpose of the relationship. Our **first** priority should be to make the relationship pleasing to God. God's standards are high and it's not always easy to meet those standards, but we should aim to reach His standards and not our own standards nor the world system standards. Most adults have been programmed to date according to the world standards and what is seen on television or heard in songs; which are usually the opposite of God's standards. This dating style usually leads too unhealthy compromise and heartache.

One of the most common unhealthy compromises you find in a love relationship is premarital sex. Don't get me wrong sex is a wonderful gift. It was instituted by God for the purpose of procreation and intimacy between a husband and his wife. I believe that once we understand the truth about premarital sex and the effects it has on our bodies and souls, we will be better able to resist the temptation. The most obvious risk of having sex nowadays are the health risk and the possibilities of contracting a sexually transmitted disease such as HIV, AIDS, Gonorrhea, or Herpes. The word teaches us to flee fornication: Flee fornication. Every sin that a man doeth is without the body; but he that committeth fornication sinneth against his own body. What? Know ye not that your body is the temple of the Holy Ghost which is in you, which ye have of God, and ye are not your own? For ye are bought with a price: therefore glorify God in your body, and in your spirit, which are God's. 1 Corinthians 6:18-20

I know you're thinking, "I hear you, and I understand what the Bible is saying; but how do I refrain from sex"? If you are in a relationship now and are currently having sex, I know that it can be extremely difficult to renew your mind and even harder to beat your body into submission to stop having sex. Of course, I am not saying it is going to be easy, but with commitment, communication, prayer, a change in your dating habits and the strength of the Lord it can be accomplished. One thing to remember is that having sex is a choice. We have to make difficult choices every day. You and your mate should meditate on the following scriptures:

> Know ye not that the unrighteous shall not inherit the kingdom of God? Be not deceived: **neither fornicators**, nor idolaters, nor

adulterers, nor effeminate, **nor abusers of themselves with mankind.** Nor thieves, nor covetous, nor drunkards, nor revilers, nor extortioners, shall inherit the kingdom of God. (bold is mine).
—1 Corinthians 6:9-10

Flee fornication. Every sin that a man doeth is without the body; but he that committeth fornication sinneth against his own body....
I Corinthians 6:18

The above scriptures states that your body is not your own but the Lord's. 1 Corinthians 6:18 says that when you commit fornication, you are sinning against your own body. 1 Corinthians 6:9 teaches us that neither fornicators nor abusers of themselves will inherit the kingdom of God. When you are fornicating, you are sinning and abusing your own body, and therefore, you will not inherit the kingdom of God! That sounds scary and it is but it is the judgment of God. The good news is God provides opportunities for us to repent and turn away from sin and be restored back into right relationship with Him. 1 Corinthians 6:11, states that such as all of us were sinners and unworthy of the inheritance of the kingdom, before we knew God and repented. Which simply means turn away from sin and God will forgive you.

We need to be de-programmed from the world system way of dating. This can only be accomplished by the power of the Holy Spirit. You must allow the Holy Spirit to restrain you. Some desire to have a relationship that is pleasing to God but do not know how to obtain it. Some lack self-discipline. Some are new to the kingdom and have not yet been equipped to refrain from the temptation of the flesh. Some do not know how to express love or affection without having sex. Some simply do not desire to have a nonsexual relationship. This may be extremely difficult for some people but we must know that all things are possible with Christ (Matthew 19:26). We must first set our hearts and minds to do the right thing: only date/court people who also want this same type of relationship, and stay out of situations that could lead to sex (e.g., dating from the house alone, spending the night, and vacationing together). You know your triggers so try to avoid those things that set you off. It takes great commitment, prayer and patience to accomplish this way of dating, especially after dating or courting for a while and are in love with each other. Be honest with yourself and your mate about your desire to wait until marriage. Do not get involved with someone who says he or she doesn't want to wait for marriage to have sex. If you are a person who is not willing to wait for marriage, then don't date someone who is trying to wait, because you could easily cause that person to fall.

Please know that I am not trying to be unrealistic, super religions or make this sound easy because it's not. Sometimes even with our best intentions we fall short because no one is without sin! Not that it's a license to live a life of sin. We need a heart and the desire to do what is right and make the choices that are best for us and based on the truth of the word of God.

We should not make choices out of fear, unhealthy compromise or desperation. After you have turned your heart to God, He will bless you and renew your mind, spirit and body so that you are able to obtain this goal of not compromising your place in the Kingdom of God. Then just as I pray, one day you will meet someone and ask the Lord, "Okay, Lord, what is your will for this relationship?" And the Lord will say something like:

> Son, this is your rib that I took out of your side and made her your wife. She has been anointed to cover your most vital organs, your heart and lungs. She will bruise the head of the enemy on your behalf. She will help birth out purpose and

destiny in your life. Take her love her, cherish her, be prosperous, and grow with her!

So too, one day after you meet Mr. Forever, you will begin to seek God's face about him. The Lord will say something like:

> Daughter, this is your king that I have given to you as a gift from me. He will love you, cherish you, protect you, and be the head over you. He will speak life into you and will help you to prosper and birth out great purpose and destiny in your life.

After reading this chapter, if you notice that you are dealing with spirits of desperation do not be discouraged and do not feel condemned. Know that greater is He (God) that is in you than he (the spirit of desperation) that is against you. God has given you all power and authority over the enemy and the enemy must flee, if you resist him.

In conclusion, know that God will answer you when you seek Him with your whole heart. Do not be afraid to know the will of God from the start. He knows the plans that He has for you and He will hearken unto you. Jeremiahs 29:11-13

Chaotic Relationship

We all know what a chaotic relationship looks like. If not, let me paint the picture for you; its driving pass his or her house to see if another car is parked in the driveway or to see if they are at home. Going by the place where your mate said they were going to be to make sure their there. Getting the code to their voice mail (of course without their knowledge) and checking their voice messages, text messages, calling back phone numbers. Some have gone as far as getting GPS on their mates phone and tracking their whereabouts (again, without their knowledge). Doing all this to feed their own insecurities, while driving their mate crazy.

If you are truly seeking a healthy relationship then you have to leave the drama behind. A lot of drama is caused by the misconception of what makes a relationship work. The world's theory is that you have to live with the person before you marry them in order to know if you can live peacefully together. It also promotes sampling the sex beforehand in order to know if you will be compatible in the bedroom. You must be able to discern a healthy relationship from a chaotic relationship. Also be aware of certain attitudes and behaviors that lead to chaotic relationships and attitudes and behaviors that lead to healthy relationships.

If you are in a chaotic relationship, you must first examine yourself and then situation. If it is you, then you need to work on you, but if it's simply not a relationship that can grow into anything good, you must be willing to let it go and move on. Sometime things that we continue to do such as not trusting him or her or double-checking everything he or she says can become life time habits that are hard to break. When you get into a relationship that actually has potential, you may bring bad habits from that chaotic relationship into the new relationship.

If you are ever going to be happy in a relationship, you must leave the drama and bad habits behind you. You must free your minds from those things. So that you are able to have a drama-free relationship and help your mate reach their goals.

Renewal to Get to My Promise

In all that I have said, please remember that there will be trials, tests, triumphs and failures, before you get the blessings of God. But anything worth having is worth waiting for and working for. It's almost comical to me when you are trying to do the right thing and live right, seems like the people around you, people who can care less about doing the right thing are getting the very thing that you want.

While others are progressing in their life and relationships you seem to be taking the scenic route to get to your heart desires. But God is still good. In fact, I have come to realize that because God took you on the scenic route to work things out in you your union, your blessings, whatever it is you are believing God for will be greater than you imagined! I believe because God took the time to prepare you for the blessings you will enjoy and appreciate them more. That said, I have to confess that I sometimes get upset when I see couples coming together all around me and I think to myself, *I am more prepared to be in a relationship than they are*, but God has a way of bursting our little bubbles.

Let me give you a few examples. One of my friends recently got married. Her and her guy dated a long time ago and then got back together about a year ago. They moved in together and were dating exclusively. Neither of them was attending church services or thinking about having a relationship that was pleasing to God, but they were happy and were talking about getting married, which they did eventually.

Another one of my girlfriends met a guy and had only been dating him for about four months when he started talking about marrying her. They went out looking for rings. Now, she was saved (although not actively going to church), but he wasn't. From the way he talked, I am not sure that he even believed in God. He ended up proposing to her, and soon after they were happily married and moved to Atlanta.

Consequently, I thought, *okay, God, something is wrong with this picture neither one of them are seeking you like I am seeking you and worshipping you like I am. They weren't even going to church! Lord, I know if they can get someone, I should be able to get someone and not have to go through this long process of learning how to be a wife. Neither of them went through it and they do not know what being a wife is all about.*

What I learned is if you are asking God for His best, then you must be right to receive the best. He will not give His pearls to pigs! He will not give His best to a person who is not fit for the best. (Although, God can do whatever He wants to do, because in the Bible, He did have a man of God marry a prostitute, but God still got the glory!) After I saw my girlfriends continue to get engaged and married, I started comparing myself to them, and of course, I thought that they weren't ready for marriage- I, however, was. We sometimes do not see ourselves or recognize our hidden issues—our attitudes, bad habits, hidden unforgiveness in our hearts, our strongholds. At thirty years old, I was unmarried, not dating, and growing impatient. So I started praying and said to God, "*If Terrance* (this guy that I liked) *is to be my husband then he has to come and get me or else I am going to be the last to get married, if ever.*" He and I were not working out the way I had hoped. I decided to go into fasting and prayer for him because I thought the problem was with him and not me. I thought God had already done the spiritual work in me to be a wife and although I had grown spiritually my promise still seemed far off. I told my friend that "*if he was to be my husband, then I was going to fight for him in the spirit realm and fast and pray that God bring us together*". On Sunday, the pastor prayed over me and said that, "God was sending me someone and that He was preparing the right person for me. He asked, "What makes you think that He is not going to give you the desires of your heart? The work is in *you*"! I was shocked that the work was still in me! All that I had been through—practicing abstinence, periods of loneliness, my unwavering faith. Through all of that, I still needed more work? *My God, I must be a complete train wreck*, I thought…

    I did fast and pray, but for myself, asking God to reveal and fix anything that would hinder me from my husband coming—and coming now! God began to reveal things to me about myself that I did not realize. He revealed one thing to me through an old boyfriend. For some reason, this ex was calling me and wanted to see me. I agreed to go see him and as we were watching television we starting talking about our relationship then he said that I seemed uncomfortable being with him as if I pushed him away once I realized that he really liked me. Of course, I dismissed what he was saying right away.

    Later, maybe midmorning around 3:00 or 4:00 AM, God woke me up and said, "Victor is right. You become afraid of men and relationships. When you notice that someone cares about you or loves you, you run the opposite direction. You put up a wall to stop them from loving you." He reminded me of all the times that I'd done that and how a wall had gone up each time. God said, "You're walls are as tall as the sky," and I could see them like a field of brick walls lined up in rows. God said, "This is not from Me it's a stronghold that you have made for yourself." In order for Him to give me what He had promised me, I would have to let all that go and trust Him. He then continued to reveal to me that, "I was a good thing and I deserve to be loved and to give love." God said, "I had forgiving them for hurting me, but I still was carrying around the hurt in my heart." He mentioned how I fed off relationships that I knew were not going anywhere, because they were safe, and that those relationships made the walls stronger. I had to cut them off. He said, "This is not from Me and I cannot take you where I want you to go with all this stuff." I didn't realize that I was hindering God from blessing me by trying to protect myself from being hurt. When I woke up I asked for forgiveness and began confessing my wrong to the Lord. I asked the Lord, *to destroy every stronghold in my life and take down every wall in the name of Jesus Christ.*

I realized that in all the times I've planned my wedding in my mind it is amazing that I have not been able to actually see myself married to anyone. I never felt that anyone was really good enough for me to marry and vice versa.

Maybe what I have just stated sounds familiar to you and if it does sound familiar do as I did and ask God to search you and give you revelation of any hindering behaviors that you may have in your life. Ask Him to renew your mind and spirit and help you to overcome every bad experience, every heartbreak, every disappointment and any feelings of rejection.

You cannot carry all of those issues around in your heart. My motto is that the enemy doesn't have to rob us because we are robbing ourselves of the desires of our hearts by not seeking God and trusting Him to prepare us for greater blessings. Don't be afraid to have the Father search you and renew your mind and spirit because everything He has for you is good, perfect, and acceptable. I thank God every day, and I will continue to seek His face for direction in my life and purge me of anything that is hindering me in my life. I don't know where this path will take me, but I will trust that my husband is coming and that I will be even more prepared for him mentally, physically, and spiritually.

I believe that God is preparing me to be a virtuous wife and mother. I thank God for getting me out of the wilderness and guiding me toward the promises He has made me. It's not that God fails us but we fail to trust Him and allow Him to mold us. I think it's because we do not like to be tested or stretched. We put ourselves into bondage with fear and a lack of forgiveness and we are unwilling to examine ourselves, so that we can see who we truly are. Allow God to search your heart and break down every stronghold and wall that is preventing you from getting the promises of God.

The Test

Okay, now here is the test! I was introduced to a minster. He was thirty-two years old and had two daughters from a previous marriage. It took me about four days to call him, because I knew I did not want to date a preacher. I called, and he explained to me how he dates. He only goes on group dates and if God does not reveal to him right away that she was his wife, then he would end the relationship. I agreed with some of his dating practices. However, I was not down with the group dating. Practically, because you cannot really get to know a person if others are always around. I was thinking *hopefully he had enough self-control to go out on a date without feeling the need to have sex. He was a minister, after all!* I thought that he was a little extreme with the dating thing but it must be because he was a minister, I was not there yet with the total group dating thing. The conversation ended with me saying, *Oh, okay, then give me your e-mail address and I will invite you to some of my church functions.* I guess he got the picture because the next day he called me and broke down his dating practices again. My mind had not changed. I understood but I was not interested. (Of course, I did not say that but I was thinking it.) God began to work on me and told me to look at it from a spiritual standpoint and not a carnal standpoint. So I began to try and see how what he was saying was beneficial and would not give room to sin- so I agreed to his dating practices. He invited me to his church to hear him preach. I went and he preached a really good message. We talked on the phone for a few weeks before going out. He asked me out on a date but could not find anyone to go out with us. Finally however, we went to dinner and horseback riding by ourselves. We never could find anyone to group date with us so we continued to date alone. He was a nice guy who loved the Lord and I enjoyed his conversation. I felt that we were making a good connection and it was fun hanging out with him.

One day while out to dinner, we were talking and laughing and all of a sudden he began to speak in tongues. At first I thought he was joking but he continued doing this throughout the night. As we continued dating it became worse and he became very religious. I was struggling to determine whether I was going to continue seeing him. My view at that time was -God helped me get over the minister thing and the group dating thing, but the speaking in tongues for no reason was going to drive me crazy! Speaking in tongues was his way of communicating with God and should not be used in a conversation with others. I believe that if it was truly the Holy Spirit leading him to speak in tongues, it would not allow him to do it out of order. I began to distance myself from him and only talked to him on the phone. I was unsure of what was going on and I had never met anyone like him before. One day we were on the phone he read me poetry, which was really romantic. At the end of the conversation, he said, "Marlena, I love you". I felt it in my bones. I thought to myself *"Oh my God, is this my husband?"* But it became too much too soon for me. I got scared and really needed to take time to talk with the Lord on this matter.

The more I prayed the more God began to reveal things to me. The more he and I talked the more things became clear to me what the Lord was telling me about the friendship and the purpose of the friendship. One of the things that resonated the most about him was he used God as a way out of relationships and he persuaded women that what he was saying was right by God's standards when really it was his own desires and thoughts. I noticed this when he was talking about an old relationship in which they loved each other. But it turned out that he had left her cold turkey! I could not understand how he could just walk away without a reason. He said, "God did not reveal to me that she was my wife." I immediately thought *"if he had sought God earlier, then He would have revealed that fact to both of them before it had gotten to a place of love."*

What I had believed to hear from God regarding him was confirmed during one of the last conversations we had; he tried to convince me that what I had heard from the Lord about my life was not true. He said this because what I shared with him about what I believed was the direction and purpose of my life, which did not line up with where his life was heading. He got very manipulative and he might have convinced me otherwise; however, I had already prayed and I was not emotional about the situation but very clear in what the Lord had spoken to me about this relationship. Now this man spoke so eloquently that I started to second guess myself at one point. I recall thinking to myself, m*aybe I am wrong and he was right? What if he was my husband and I was missing out by still holding onto my own desires?*

With these doubts I called my pastor and told him what was going on and asked him for his thoughts. He was very encouraging and he mentioned how I should read the Book of Ruth. He said that God had a Boaz for me and that if there was no peace in that relationship or the thought of being with him, then maybe he was not the one. Maybe we needed to take more time before we made any big decisions about our relationship. I read the story of Ruth and began to understand what he had meant about God having a Boaz for me. (Read the Book of Ruth it will encourage you to.)

I also called my cousin, a powerful woman of God and a Pastor. She said that, "although we as humans make mistakes I needed to protect my anointing." I did not know that I had an anointing.

I called them because I needed advice—and Godly advice not worldly advice. It's always wise to seek counsel from mature women and men of God. Whether you talk to your pastor, minister, or deacons, elders in the church or your family that you can trust and who will not spread your business, those who will pray with you and give you good advice.

Eventually, I learned that I did have an anointing to protect and that God was sending me someone who would love me and not try to manipulate me with the word of God for his own purposes. I learned that we must know God for ourselves, because there are some people who know the word of God and use it for their own benefit; to manipulate and take advantage of others. I say that because during some of those long night conversations with the minister, I had to stand up for who I was in Christ and say what I believed to be the truth for my walk of faith with the Lord.

As we grow and mature as Christians the enemy cannot use the same kind of man or woman to tempt us. Now he is sending people who appear to know God—and they very well might have a relationship with God—but that doesn't mean that you should marry that person. Be ready to stand firm in your beliefs, and protect your anointing. We all have an anointing on our lives. We may not be aware of it but if you have been born again in Christ Jesus, you are a new creature. God lives in you and He has anointed you to fulfill His purpose and His will! (We will talk more about anointing later in the book.)

Off Path of My Promise

As mentioned several times before, the road to doing things the right way may seem longer or may have more hills, curves, and rocky terrain. It's that way because God has prepared something great for you and you must build character to be able to handle the blessings. Sometimes, it appeared that I was faced with challenges that had nothing to do with preparing me to be a wife. For example, God has been using me to minister to others about things going on in their lives. In my mind, it is nowhere near where I desire to be, which is closer to the promise of marriage and teaching me how to be a wife. As a matter of fact, the anointing on my life leads me to be encouraging and happy for others who are getting exactly what I want, while encountering people who don't appreciate it or are not giving thanks to God for their blessings. One particular situation that comes to mind happened with my male friend. In one of our conversations he told me that while he was talking with his fiancée, he mentioned to her that if he hadn't met me and talked with me about God and the Bible, he wouldn't be prepared to be with her. After hearing that my first thought was *Glory to God*! With this relationship, both of them loved God and were trying to have a relationship that was pleasing to Him. They prayed together and went to church together. They abstained from sex until they were married. This was a blessed relationship from the beginning, because they were making God the center of their relationship and were looking to Him for guidance. Their relationship brought honor to God, who is always pleased with us when we give Him honor and glory. A Christian relationship should be different from a carnal (worldly) relationship. As Christians, we should not be living together, having sex, or acting crazy with all kinds of cursing and foolishness. We should be able to talk through disagreements and misunderstandings with love and patience. All that being said- I am sincerely thankful to God for giving me the words and ability to encourage my friends, but this still brings me (in my mind) no closer to my promise!

One day, I was talking with a friend, and the word from God to me for her was, "She needs to find her way back to Him." Now her deal is-she is living in her promise yet still unhappy and is missing out on the fullness of God's blessings, because she is out of fellowship with Him. She and I have been friends for a while. Actually, she encouraged me to start reading and trying to understand the Bible. We have been through some of the same similar things—babies at a young age, baby daddy drama, school for ten years for four-year degrees, full-time work during part-time school, struggles with men and relationships, and raising children on our own.

Finally, God allowed her to graduate from law school and move to Florida, making a six-figure salary. A good guy who wants to marry her—did I mention he was a doctor?—he moved to Florida to be closer to her in a matter of weeks. She now has everything I can remember her asking for. Guess what? Can you believe she is still not happy? Why? Because she is out of fellowship with God. She is missing out on the joy of all the hard work she's put into school and now having a wonderful man who loves her and her child. I have to comfort and encourage her because she is messing up. *"Why do I have to keep encouraging her when she has everything she has ever wanted?"* I thought to myself. But God blessed me so that I could set aside my desires and encourage her and tell her the truth about her situation. I love my friend, and I want her to be happy while she is living in her promise. I didn't originally think that this situation was a test but it was, God wanted to know if I could be a true friend when they got what I desired.

The biggest test for me was when Victor called me and I had to encourage him about his new girlfriend. I was trying to speak wisdom into him about holding on to her and being patient. In the past I was in love with him, and he never reciprocated love back to me. Instead he dangled me around for over a year ultimately confessing that he had been seeing someone else. He was trying to get rid of me, but I wouldn't leave and I didn't give him what he needed. That hurt like nothing before, and it took God himself and a bunch of tears and prayers to heal me from that relationship. Now, however, God was using me to help him with his relationship with another woman. I didn't know her or her side of the story, but I recognized the spirit that she had and how it was screaming for healing. She was treating him badly because of what had happened to her in past relationships. As I listened to him talk about their problems, I knew that they both needed to bring God into their relationship and allow Him to heal those past hurts.

We often miss out on what God has for us, because we are not renewed in our mind and spirits. Their relationship reminded me a lot of myself (before my renewal process had begun). For example, in the past, if the guy was not doing what *I* thought he should be doing in the time frame that *I* thought was appropriate then all hell would break loose! *I* was always bringing to light the things he did wrong and wouldn't listen to what *I* was doing wrong to him. When *I* did notice it, *I* would say, *"Oh, I am working on it"* but I never sought God for change. Eventually, the relationship would end. Notice I kept saying "I." That is the problem because there is no "I" in a relationship. It's both of you, and both of you have feelings and desires. It's two people trying to be one in mind, body and spirit. If your mindset is all about what you want and how you want it, the relationship will not last long. Learn to give as well as receive.

Although, I thought I was off my path to be renewed for marriage, I was not. I learned valuable lessons through helping others and then taking a look at myself. I noticed in relationships were God is included; they are happy and progressing not without issues but working through those issues in a Christian manner. The relationships that disregard God altogether are unhappy and struggling at the very basic level of the relationship. As a result, those relationships probably will not last long. You do the math!

The experiences above finally made sense to me one day when my friend came to my house. As we were conversing I said, "I did not understand when women said they didn't need a man. "I have a list of things I need a man to do for me." He responded, "I see what you mean." He then told me that when he walked in my house he thought "this girl needs a man". Not that my house is torn down or terribly dirty, but he probably felt that lonely spirit. Later, God revealed to me that day that it was not by chance that I didn't have a man at that time in my life. He made me depend on Him for what I would have depended on a man to do instead. I had to learn to lean and trust Him for what I needed. That was so profound to me, because it was so true. I would have just asked my man for money if I needed some. I would have called my man over or went out on a date on lonely nights instead of praying and reading my Bible and worshipping God. This time alone allowed me to develop my relationship with God, and I hadn't realized it until that day. If it hadn't been for this season in my life, I would have been like others who are living in their promise and not enjoying it because they don't have a personal relationship with Christ. If you are alone right now and desire to be married, spend this time with God. On those Friday or Saturday nights when you would normally be out on a date pick up your Bible or just worship God in song. You don't have to ask for anything but just rest in His presence. Trust Him to give you what you need. You will be amazed at the breakthrough you get in your mind and spirit. The peace that passes all understanding is real!

Pressing Through

Whether you're challenged with raising children, financial issues, work, sickness, drama with friends or family, or just breaking up with your significant other I strongly suggest you stay strong and keep your eyes on the prize, which is Christ Jesus and His will for your life. We pray for blessings, and God makes us promises, know that God has the power to do what He has promised. Romans 4:21

Allow God to prepare you for your husband or wife or whatever it is that you have asked for or that God has promised you. Be prepared to fight tooth and nail for the promises of God and for those things you have asked Him to do in your life. When waiting for those blessing to manifest, it's then that God prepares you for the blessing. What I have discovered is that God sends a test before the blessings. He prepares you for the test during those quiet times in your life which I call the -preparation season. Look at it this way: During the winter, the trees are bare. Nothing is growing, but something is going on at the roots. When the spring comes, the trees begin to produce. It's the same way with you. God is preparing you during the quiet season of your lives. He is planting a seed of growth, renewal, wisdom, and patience. Whatever you have been praying for, God is planting seeds through the experiences, times of quietness, loneliness, trials and tribulations. During the right time these seeds will produce fruit. Let's say the fruit is a relationship. We say, "Bless you, Jesus. I have finally gotten what I have been asking you for!" Then in the middle of us enjoying the fruit the test comes.

My test came and I only remember thinking, *I thought I was over this. I thought I was delivered from this issue.*

God said, "No, my daughter, I have been preparing you to handle this situation when it comes back up again." He wanted to see if I was going to fall back into my old ways or deal with this in a Christian manner.

What are you going to do when the test comes? What are you going to do when God has prepared you to be in a Christian relationship and you find yourself in one? What if you want to have sex with this person, what are you going to do? What if they piss you off what are you going to say? What if they make a mistake, are you going to forgive them? All I can say is don't give up, if you mess up during the test just acknowledge your wrong to God and keep trying.

To pass your test you must stand and fight with what God has given you during that season of quietness. He has placed an awesome power in you and now you have to put what you have learned into practice. I experienced this first-hand. I was dating this guy and issues began to come up things that I thought I had conquered during my quiet season. Issues I thought I would not have to deal with once I was in a Christian relationship—the temptation of sex, arguments, disagreements, selfishness and other issues.

At first, I begin to cry like a baby and wanted to just give up, but my friend reminded me, that I was prepared to deal with these issues in the right way. That God had prepared me to pass this test. I prayed and asked God to show me how to handle these issues. I was reminded not to allow the enemy to rob me of an opportunity to give love and receive love. At this time, I knew who Jesus was to me and who I was in Christ Jesus. I knew that I did not have to sit and cry like a baby or run like a coward or even give into my flesh. So I became determined not to go back to my old ways that were detrimental to the relationship. Instead we sat down and talked through our disagreement rather than arguing and saying things that we would later regret. I actually listened to him and tried to do better versus giving up without trying. He and I broke up but it was not because I did not handle myself appropriately, it was not because of sin or because of me having a carnal mind set. But he was there to help me learn a lesson, he was there as a test.

What Is the Reason for the Relationship Anyway?

Most relationships in our lives are there for a reason. We have brothers, sisters, aunts, mothers, and fathers. In short, we usually know the reason for the relationship. It's different for an intimate relationship between a man and woman, sometimes you are not clear the reason for the relationship. Whether this person is there for a season, a life time, whether they are there to teach you something, give you something or hinder you from something. It helps to know the reason for the relationship and your responsibility is to make sure it brings glory and honor to God.

This is something I struggle with because, to be honest, my first thought when I meet a nice guy is, *is he my husband*? But I am learning that this mindset is not healthy mentally or emotionally. Because of my mindset I have completely missed the opportunity to minister to someone, or develop a lasting friendship. I have been so focused on being married at certain times that I have completely missed the mark. God spoke to me and said, *marriage is much more than what you see on the surface*. It's not just about being married for the sake of saying you're married. The ultimate goal is not to have two incomes and a big house, it's not just about cooking and cleaning and material things. But it is a gift from God. It's about two people coming together to bring glory to God. The love that should be displayed in a marriage is a depiction of the love God has for His people.

I have discovered that marriage is about serving. Marriage is about sacrificing for the love of someone else. Marriage is about friendship. Marriage is hard work. Marriage is so many things that I can't name it all. But know that it is not all about you!

But don't get discouraged because while marriage is not like the fairy tales we read as little children. It is actually greater! God has created and ordained a relationship between a man and a woman that is like no other relationship on earth. But don't just take my word for it, seek God for yourself and ask Him what is marriage?

So I will ask you, if you are in an intimate relationship, ask yourself what is the reason for this relationship? What is my motive do I really want to fulfil God's purpose or my own?

In conclusion, I know a lot of you reading this book may be in relationships, perhaps long-term relationships. Probably, relationships that started before you were saved or before you began desiring to do things God's way. You may not even be saved but if God is drawing your heart and you desire to be in a relationship that fulfils God's purpose, the first step is to ask God in prayer what's the reason for the relationship? Next talk with your mate and ask them their thoughts about the purpose of the relationship and do they think it's accomplishing what God wants it to accomplish. If you discover that the relationship has not been bringing glory and honor to God, it's not too late to turn it around. It may not be easy to change the relationship but know that with God all things are possible.

Pour Into Me

I have learned some very hard lessons on this journey of being taught how to be a wife. This particular situation broke me.

There was a guy my friend wanted me to meet. However, she did not want to directly hook us up. She had a dinner at her house and invited us and a few other people over hoping that something would spark between the two of us. He and I began to talk throughout the night about work and kids, mutual people we knew from high school because we went to rivaling high schools. We exchanged phone numbers and he called me the next day. We talked for a while had very good conversations. As time went on I began to like him.

It was prophesied that I was going to marry a minister. During the course of us talking I found out that it was prophesied to him that he was going to be a minister. I immediately thought "is *this my husband*?" That little piece of information made me like him more.

Later my girlfriend told me that she had a dream that he and I were going to be married. Then my sister had a similar dream that he and I were getting married. Later in the month another one of my friends called and said, "She had a dream that I was getting married wearing I beautiful white dress and everyone was so happy." She said, "The dream was so real she thought that it was really happening."

Needless to say I was sure these were signs from the Lord that he was my future husband. I began to pray for us and I completely dismissed the fact that we never went out on dates and only talked on the phone and he we come over and we will stay up late talking and having fun with each other. I figured he was taking his time to get to know me and that it will all work out so I was extremely patient. This went on for about a year and a half. I truly believed he was my husband and I was willing to wait. I prayed for him daily for over a year and was convinced he was the one.

One day I called him and he was on his way to the airport I asked who he was picking up and he said a girl's name. He went onto to explain that he reunited with a lady that he use to date in college and she was in town for the weekend. He said, "I believe she is my future wife". I was hurt I did not know what to say. Truthfully, I could not say anything because we were not in a committed relationship.

That night I prayed and cried and was angry with God. I could not understand why God would let me go for over a year believing he was my husband! I had been pouring out my spirit into him through prayer and fasting and once it became evident that he was not going to be my husband, I felt empty!

I know that this story sounds extreme, and you're probably wondering why she would let this go on for a year with him not committing to her? Well, when you believe something with all your heart, you respond according to that belief.

I was hurt for a long time and could hardly pray. I was angry with God, myself, and my heart was broken. After a while of feeling this way, I allowed God to comfort me. God showed me that I was in error; I should have gotten a clear answer from Him before going that deep into prayer in fasting for someone. God revealed to me that I was acting out of my own desires and that my friends and sister may have dreamed about us getting married but that was all it was, a dream.

There was so much I learned from this situation. The main thing is that God loves me! He is a healer for those who are broken. He is able to renew us and restore us even when we are in error. I learned that love is not an emotion love is an action. That action should not leave you feeling empty.

Finally, when we pray for people we are pouring our anointing, our spirits, and energy into them. We are allowing the enemy to come into our lives, because we are standing in the gap for this person. However, before we start pouring our spirits into others with a certain expectation we should make sure that our expectation is in God's will for our lives. It is important to pour out to others but we should make sure that they are also pouring into us. Relationships are give and take. We should not always be taking and we should not always be giving. There should be a balance in what you pour out and what you receive. If your pouring out to others in prayer, love and patience, I hope that person is pouring into you prayer, love, and patience or whatever it is you need from them. Looking back I would not change anything however, I do not plan to make that mistake again. I now seek God's will first through prayer and fasting before I begin to pour my anointing, energy and time into people with a certain expectation. Don't get me wrong I pray for people that I date but I pray asking God's will to be manifested in our lives. That if this person is to be my husband let it be confirmed with both of us.

Looking Beyond the Situation to See God

Remember that I am sharing this book with you as I am too taking this journey of renewing my mind and spirit so that I will not forget small details after God takes me into my promise. At this point my mind has become too distracted wondering who is going to be my husband and when will he come. I can't hear from God because of my own thoughts, anxieties and the problem with that is, He is the only one who can get me to where I need to be so that I can be ready for my husband. During this time my friend Martha called and she could see better than me what was going on, she was encouraging and helped me get back on track by reminding who I am in Christ and what I need to be doing. I couldn't see the forest for the tree. I truly needed to be in the presence of God so that He could renew my strength in Him. Now, I am truly setting my emotions and desires at God's feet and leaving them there. Understand that I am not losing hope of marriage but giving it to God and releasing it to Him.

Cast thy burden upon the Lord, and he shall sustain thee. He shall never suffer the righteous to be moved. —Psalms 55:22

    I figure in order to be ready to move when God says move, I have to hear and know His voice. I can only hear His voice when I am available to hear. I am available to hear when I am not tied down with my own thoughts and emotions.

How will you know if it's God and not your own feelings and emotions speaking? You first must know God and His word and be able to discern the spirit behind your thoughts and feelings. You have to be willing to bottle up all your feelings and emotions and put them under the submission of the Holy Spirit. This will be hard in the beginning, but the more you do it, the easier it will become. I usually begin by asking myself a few questions to determine the spirit behind my thoughts and emotions. I asked myself how do I feel right now?

- *Am I feeling anxious*
- *confused*
- *obsessed*
- *desperate*
- *fearful*
- *Am I truly letting God move or am I moving*
- *What does the word of God say about this subject*

When you are in a situation and can't hear God's voice, begin to take steps to first remove yourself from the situation emotionally so that you can hear clearly from God and not become distracted by your own thoughts and emotions:

I would suggest physically removing yourself from the situation if at all possible. For example, stay off the phone talking about the situation even if it's for a couple of hours, know it does not take God all day to do anything.

1. Pray. Ask God to silence every voice that is not His.
2. Ask for wisdom and guidance in the situation.
3. Then ask Him one question and wait for the answer. For

example, you may ask, "Lord, what is your will for me in this situation?"
4. If you don't hear anything, stay there as long as you can wait for Him to answer and just praise and worship Him until He answers.

In some cases, God may not answer you. He may just want you to trust Him but there are times when He will answer you and you should obey.

In saying all of that, communication is a wonderful thing and you should let your partner know that you will be unavailable for however long you choose to consecrate yourself to God. I believe a true man or woman of God will understand this and should keep you lifted in prayer even joining you in prayer.

I did exactly what I said and fasted and prayed with my emotions in check but I didn't hear anything from God. I have continued to move on with my life believing that God's plan for me is perfect and will be revealed to me in His own time and season. Although I did not hear God say anything about who my husband was or when he was coming He did give me peace in my emotions and mind. He strengthened my spirit so that I could wait without being anxious. In my heart, I know that I am being prepared for marriage and to be a virtuous wife and mother. God has told me that I will exceed them all! If you are in the same situation or a similar one and you find that you are too emotional about a situation, know that things happen in the spirit first and then manifest later by faith through grace. Look beyond your current circumstance and see God moving on your behalf.

Worship

So many Christians and non-Christians are searching for their purpose in life, the reason for their existences on earth. Although some people will disagree with me, it is not a secret. We were created in God's image for His good pleasure, to worship Him, and to build up the Kingdom of God! Before Lucifer was thrown out of heaven he was the worship leader (Isaiah 14:12–15) and we have taken the place of Lucifer, God created man in His own image to worship him. However, God does not force us to worship Him-He gives us the choice on whether we will worship Him or not.

Because so many people don't know this very simple truth they are struggling to please God. When the only thing we can truly give God is our worship. I believe that this lack of knowledge is why so many Christians are not maturing in the faith and not being empowered for Christ.

True worship does not depend on how you feel. It is not determined by your situation or your troubles. True worship is not held off until you get to the church building on Sunday. True worship comes from knowing who God is. When you know and understand the great sacrifice Christ made for you, you no longer allow others, situations, troubles, trials, good times or bad times determine how and when you worship Him. When you get a small grasp of who He is and what He did for you, you realize that all you can do to please Him is to worship Him.

When I try to conceptualize what Christ did for me, I become overwhelmed! For those who don't know what am speaking about, I will give you a tiny glimpse of what He did. Christ being God, left His heavenly home to be born of a woman, to become a flesh and blood man, only to be mistreated, misunderstood, rejected and beaten, hung naked on a rugged cross with the pain of nails in His hands and feet, He suffered without complaining, not because He deserved it. No it should have been you; it should have been me in His place. But Christ did all of that, because He loves us, because He is love.

Hopefully, that tiny depiction of what Christ did for us and who He is, will have you come to the same conclusion that I have, He deserves our worship.

Some of the saints in the Bible had to have understood who Christ was and their purpose in life. There are amazing stories throughout the Bible were the saints of God worshipped Him, simply because He deserved their worship and when they worshipped, miraculous things happened! In the book of Acts, Paul and Silas were beaten badly and then thrown into prison. They did not murmur or complain asking why them but they began to praise and worship God in spite of their pain and suffering. Look at what God did- God loosened the chains that were binding them in the natural and in the spiritual. Others who were jailed saw how these men loved God and they also believed in God and were saved and baptized. I am sure that the disciples' faith increased when God moved on their behalf as a result of their worship and praise unto Him. If you could learn to worship Him despite your circumstances I believe that God would begin to change things for your good as well and that your faith in Him will increase. I believe that God would begin to loosen the chains that bind you and loose that which he has ordained for you since the foundation of the earth was formed. If you are not experiencing the glory of God like these saints in the Bible, I dare you to tap into the power of worship! I dare you to truly seek to find out who God is!

Some Christians have not tapped into the power that God has given them through their worship, because they have not yet learned the necessity of true worship. They continue to struggle with the same fears, addictions, sin, and depression- year after year there is no real change in their lives in-spite of the fact that they go to church several times a week or have been in church for many years.

Now in saying that, I am a strong believer that when the word of God is preached in truth things should change. So it is correct to attend church to hear the word of God. But there is more that must be done to receive the change that the word can and will bring.

First, come expecting and believing that God is able and willing to do the impossible. We should go to church expecting God to move in our lives, we should be anticipating experiencing His presence in the worship service. Just like Paul and Silas experienced Him while they were in prison, after they began to worship him!

Because life brings so many challenges it would be unrealistic of me to say that we should not expect God to do things for us. The truth is if God does not do it, it will not get done! However, what I have learned is, our personal desires cannot be our only motive for going to church or worshipping Him! We know that some of us only praise God because we have enough sense to know that we need Him to make a way out of trouble for us but if you praise Him only because He can get you out of trouble then I will venture to say you are not doing it with your whole heart. You are simply praising Him because you need His help. True worship as displayed by Paul & Silas comes from realizing who He is! He is God!

Let's stop right here and take an evaluation of our motives for going to church & worshipping God. Do you go to church out of tradition, to socialize, to be entertained, to be seen, to appear holy, because you are in trouble and need help to get out of trouble? Do you go to church because it is your reasonable service to God? Do you go because it is a place to be with likeminded people who also have a spring of worship and their hearts for God because of who He is? For those who have experienced the power of true worship, already know that you don't have to wait to get to the church building to worship God! You can do it at work, in the car, in your room, in the bathroom at work, you have gotten the revelation that He is God and no matter what the only thing you can do for Him is to worship Him! God creating a central place for the believers of God to gather together is a bonus especially for a single person, because the word of God has already promised that He will be present where two or three are gathered in His name He will be in the midst of them. Matthew 18:20

Whether you go to church every Sunday or only on Christmas and Easter, you can still experience the presence of God when you worship Him. Do you know the story of the ten lepers that Jesus healed? They simply asked, and He healed them; however, only one came back to worship Him, and Jesus made him whole, not just healed. This takes us to another subject about being healed and being made whole.

God created you to be whole. You are whole if you live and move in Christ Jesus the Lord. Your husband or wife does not make you whole. As much as they would want to make you whole that cannot, they can only participate in the healing process. God alone is the one whom heals and makes us whole. I am trying to convey that, God desires for you to be healed and whole in your heart, mind, emotions and spirit – today! You do not have to wait until you get into a relationship or married to feel whole! God is the only one who can make you whole. Christians sometimes feel ashamed to admit that they are broken and need healing. They do not want to admit that they are struggling with issues of past or present abuse, pain, heartache, sickness, disease, bad attitudes, bad habits, fornication, adultery, homosexuality, bisexuality and they desperately need to be made whole. But I stand as a witness that God can and will not only heal you but will make you whole in spite of your marital status or private struggles. Be like the leper and go back and worship Jesus.

The Quest for Submission

I was listening to a local radio talk show, and the topic was how black men preferred to date white women. The men were saying that black women were too argumentative, out of shape, and too independent. They mentioned all of the negative things about black women learned from their experiences. They continued the conversation, stating that they preferred white women because they were more submissive than black women. As I continued to listen, submission was the main reason mentioned for their preference.

I believe that it is okay to date outside of your race, but it is a disfranchisement to think that white women are better than black women or are more submissive as a whole. After listening to the radio talk show, it occurred to me that most people don't really know what it means to be submissive.

For centuries the principles of submission has been taught incorrectly even in the churches, many women have suffered greatly by what was supposed to be "submission". God created submission for good and not for evil. Jesus himself demonstrated the ultimate act of submission, the word of God teaches us about submission but if used for your own selfless reasons then the very mention of the word submission will cause rebellion in your home.

While submission has many dynamics we will look at submission from the perceptive of marriage and a wife's submission to her husband. One reason a wife should submit to her husband is because the Bible teaches us in Ephesians 5:22-33; Wives, submit yourselves unto your own husbands, as unto the Lord. Women are to submit to our husband as unto the Lord, meaning we submit to our husbands as we do to God. Submission means to be his helpmeet, to help him reach his goals and purpose that God created him for. Submission is allowing him to lead the household. I know this is probably making some of your cringe because you are accustom to leading your own household and leading instead of following. But if you want to be in line with the word of God then once you get married you need to let your husband lead and you submit to him. By submitting to him you will be creating an environment for God's blessing to flow.

Let's discuss what submission is not. Submission is not being treated like less of a person by your husband because he has rule over you. Submission is not being a doormat for your husband. Submission is not being verbally, emotionally, physically and spiritually abused by your husband because he has authority over you.

If you are still thinking that submission is too hard for you read what God commanded husbands to do for their wives. In, Ephesians 5:25 Husbands, love your wives, even as Christ also loved the church, and gave himself for it. I believe that this is an equally difficult task because it is not in men's first nature to "love". It however, is their first nature to lead, subdue, work, and provide. Not only must they love us but they must give themselves for us as Christ did for the Church. Just in case you don't understand what Christ gave for the church- He died!! (Philippians 2:8)

Following God's commands always lead to blessings so submitting to your husbands should not be any different. If you are struggling with this concept it's ok, but don't follow the world system way and don't submit to your husband because if you don't you will not create an environment conducive for him to strive and grow. Truth is if he can't lead in your home, he will find somewhere else to lead.

Finally, my suggestion is while you are still single learn to submit to God, as a matter of fact, submit your hopes, dreams, desires, hurts, pain, struggles, single mind-set, and your life to Christ today! I believe that when the time comes God will allow you to submit to your husband and will allow you love your wife.

Testimonies of Married Men & Women

A lot of people grew up in single parent homes and were taught to be strong and independent. Some like myself grew up in a married family but were still not taught about relationships and marriage. I have noticed that it's hard to find a married couple that will give you real advice on being married. In my experience when I have asked married couples about marriage they normally will say, "Oh it's hard". I have always thought after hearing that, *being single is hard too*. I asked some of my married friends to share and give real sound advice to those desiring to be married. I hope their advice will be as helpful to you as it was to me.

Bridget P.
Married for one year (Twenty-nine years old)

My advice to singles is to seek God and to know His plan for your life. Know who you are. Prepare yourself for marriage, and learn to trust God. Marriage is not to be taken lightly. It is a covenant between two people who have become one before God. Matthew 19:6 says, "What therefore God has joined together let no man separate." Marriage is a living symbol of Christ and the church Ephesians 5:23. Though marriage is serious, know that it is also honorable and good, and it is a joyous experience.

Seek God First and Know His Plans for You

If your heart's desire is to be married, talk to God about it. He already knows the desires of your heart. But the acknowledgment of your desires invites Him to be a part of your "plans," and it gives Him the invitation to take control of that area of your life. Ask God in prayer what His plan for your life is. Ask Him what your God-given purpose, talents, and gifts are. This gives you an opportunity to spend time with God and to explore and experience your spiritual gifts.

Prepare Yourself

It is a good to be prepared mentally, physically, and spiritually for marriage. A marriage cannot work if you are selfish. Get your mind ready to take care of your household, not just yourself. Whatever your role may be—the provider or the caregiver—you must get ready to fulfill that role. Take marriage classes. Read the Bible to discover what God's word has to say about marriage. Hang out and talk to married couples so that you can get advice or just observe their actions. Pray for yourself as well as your future spouse.

When I was single, I prayed to God about my husband before I knew who he was. I prayed for his health, his wisdom, and his spiritual growth and I thanked God for preparing him to be the husband that He had in store for me. When we choose to take on a life-changing task, we often prepare so that we can be equipped for that situation whenever it takes place. For example, we prepare for college by taking college preparatory classes. We socialize with those who are college bound. We buy scientific calculators and go to college informational sessions. We do the same when we are preparing to become a parent to our first child. So should it be the same with marriage. However, I caution you, there should be balance in everything that you do. Don't obsess over marriage and think about it more than you think about He who created it.

Know Who You Are

Know your strengths and weaknesses. Are you a good communicator? Are you honest? Are you more alert in the mornings or evening? Are you afraid of intimacy?

Are you good with finances? Do you set goals? Are you a procrastinator? We are all still growing. All Christians are a work in progress. But you should know yourself at the moment and be honest with yourself and others about who you are. Sometimes, we say we are good at something that we want to become, but we may not have arrived yet. Knowing who you are will help you know what characteristics you can accept or reject in a spouse.

Trust God

Trust God in your dating. I suggest giving every relationship the four-season test. Wait a full year. By then, you will have seen all four seasons before marriage. There is no substitution for time. In your dating, remember that you can't date as the world does, for you are a Christian. The Bible is a good place for instruction. Believe it or not, it gives instructions for dating. Stay away from the appearance of evil. Yield not to temptation. Don't have children out of wedlock, but wait on God. Remain prayerful, for God will let you know when your spouse has come. He will also let you know how to minister to him or her. When I was single, I had a list of things that I did and did not want in a husband. I posted that list on a mirror in my bedroom. The list was quite long. Then, at the very end, I wrote, "Lord, what do you want to add or take away?" Funny, isn't it? Well, God gave me what I wanted and, more importantly, what I needed. There were things on that list that I said I didn't want but my husband has. But because I *learned* to trust God, He blessed me beyond what I could have ever imagined. I am still finding out new things that I love about my husband, and I wouldn't dare take credit for him finding me or me picking him. I tell people all the time that I had nothing to do with it. God handpicked him for me, and I am glad that He did. Only God knows you better than you know yourself. Only God knows what you need now and will want ten years from now.

Trust in the Lord with all thine heart; and lean not unto thine own understanding. In all thy ways acknowledge Him, and He shall direct thy paths. Be not wise in thine own eyes: fear the Lord, and depart from evil. —Proverbs 3:5

Don't date with a wedding in mind. Think about marriage. Don't think that the person will change after marriage. Accept and love that person for who he or she is, because only God can change a person. Don't get married to prevent yourself from living a life of sin. Physical things change, but love is a strong foundation that lasts. Don't judge people by your standards. Let God lead you, which means that you will have to submit to and follow Him. Don't be afraid to discuss plans for children (e.g., discipline, finances, and health issues). We are human, and these things are all important. But know that prayer and communication are the keys to your success. Understand that whatever your strengths and weaknesses are now, they will be magnified in marriage. This happens because they are no longer just your concerns but the concerns of the one with whom you now share your life.

Ronee H.
Thirty-one years old
Married for eight years

Loosing yourself

Love your husband and your children to the deepest depth of your heart and soul. Be the rock that your husband, children, and family need you to be, but *never*—let me repeat, *never*—lose yourself in the process. Get your hair done, ladies. Get your feet done. Get a massage. Hang out with your friends. Whatever you do now that gives you peace and satisfies your soul, don't lose that thing when you get married. Don't get me wrong—you will have more things on your plate as a wife, and you will not be able to do all of the same things that you do now when you're married. Nevertheless, remember to save a little bit for yourself. As women, we tend to take on so much from husbands, children, work, church, and school, leaving nothing for ourselves. I can't tell you how, but you don't want to look up one day and wonder what happened to the person you were. After you get married, you should look in the mirror at a better you, not a person you don't recognize. Also, don't get it twisted—and I say that with the utmost respect and concern! But yes, ladies, don't *get it twisted*. You need to do those same things that you did to get your man or husband after you get him. Yes, you may gain some weight. You may go through rough times together that can't be avoided. You may not be able to do all the same things you used to do to keep it hot! However, what you must not do is use this as an excuse to look a mess! Your husband may not say that you need your hair fixed or that you're gaining weight, but you should take care of yourself nonetheless. Moreover, if you have a good husband, he will love you either way.

If you're gaining some weight, ladies, buy your clothes bigger. If your skin needs some help, go to the dermatologist or get some makeup. Whatever it is that you need to do to keep yourself up, *do it*. Don't make excuses like "oh, I'm too big" or "oh, my skin is bad" or "oh, I have to take the kids here and there." Trust me, ladies. It doesn't take much to keep yourself up if you're doing it on a regular basis. For me, it's keeping my hair fixed. This is when I'm at my best! I can throw on a pair of sweats, some tennis shoes, and a little makeup and be just as cute as I want to be! This is my thing. Find your thing that makes you feel good, and *do it*. If you're like me and getting your hair done is your thing, and you don't have money to go to the salon, find that girlfriend that can curl hair! This way you can kill two birds with one stone. You can have a good visit with your girlfriend, and you can get your hair curled in the process! It's truly about making time! Find your thing! Don't let life beat you down and lose that thing that makes you who you are, which is who your husband married, *right*? Again, marriage should make you a better you, not a worse you. If the latter is the case, something is wrong with that picture. This is also why you need that one or two *true* friends to check you. (Yes, I said check you!). I hope all of us have those girlfriends that can come to us and say, "You're being silly. Wake up. You need your hair done. Buy a bigger size in that. That's too little!" Yes, initially you might get mad, but then you have to ask yourself, "Is she right?" Only your true friends will say it and say it with love. Those same friends can also be a calming force in your life when everything appears to be going haywire. Don't lose that, ladies. Don't let go of those friendships. *Don't lose yourself.*

Submissive Wife

I do believe in being a submissive wife to my husband, letting my husband be the rightful head of our household, doing his "man thing!" But I do not believe that being submissive means being a doormat. To start, I'll tell you what I believe being submissive is not. It is not allowing your husband to walk all over you and make you feel like you're not worthy. It is not allowing your husband to put everything else in his world first before you and your family. It is not allowing your husband to have things going on outside of your home that you know nothing about. It is not being okay with how he treats you or your children if it is not with the appropriate amount of love and affection that is deserving of a wife and children.

Being submissive means showing love and respect for your husband by being supportive, understanding, and encouraging. It means being strong when he is weak, loving him in a way that he doesn't even understand, allowing room for him to be his naked self with you (sharing a piece of himself that he's never shared with anyone else). In a stronger sense, it also means calling your man on things when need be. It is your job as a wife to look out for your family, not in the same way that your husband does, but in your way. You should make sure that your house is in order and that your children are taken care of, just to name two. I'm not saying that you have to be his mother, but I am saying that some men tend to need a little extra. By extra, I mean a little extra push to make a move, and as a wife, it is your responsibility to give him that extra. Yes, ladies, we have a big job to do, but that's why you're reading this book, right? In addition, while he's constantly doing his "man thing," you have to constantly move behind the scenes.

Moving behind the scenes doing what, you may ask? You should make sure that your husband is the best man that he can be by encouraging him to never give up, apply for that new job, fix the fan in your bedroom, call the insurance company and make sure an electrician comes out, make sure to stop by the store on the way home and pick up some cheese, and be a good son to his mother by being concerned and taking an interest. The situations noted above may not be your situations, but put your situations in the place of mine and keep it moving! Yes, in my opinion, this is still being submissive while also being the wife your husband needs you to be. This is truly revealed by not letting him skirt his responsibilities, not only as a husband and a father but also as a son, uncle, and brother. Your submissiveness plants the seed in your husband's mind while you give him the time and space he needs to grow into the husband God will have him to become.

Communicating with Your Husband

Some women understandably have a meeker personality than I have, and they are probably a lot less mouthy than I tend to be at times! But what I've found is that you have to find a way of getting through to your husband in regards to the things that are important. For me, it means not beating around the bush, facing our issues head on, and letting him know. Also, I've found that it's important to share with him things like how I feel about situations—and not always the edited version! When I'm good or sad or I'm having a good day or bad day (which is sometimes more often than not!), he will know. Be truthful and up front with your husband. This is your husband. Who better to let know how you feel than him? You cannot call your girlfriends, gripe, and moan about what's going on in your household when you haven't addressed it with the only other person who can change the situation—your husband! Ladies, we have to "women up" and speak our minds not nag but in an adult manner communicate openly with him. Do not allow your feelings to be hurt or your day become worrisome without telling your husband. My friend once told me, "Your husband can speak life into your situation". This truly resonated in my spirit teaching me about how my husband could say a few words and make my day brighter or make me more at ease. Be real. Keeping things to yourself is what you do when you're dating, but you're not dating anymore. This is the man you are planning to spend the rest of your life with. *Woman up!*

<u>Having God in Your Lives</u>

And lastly, I would be totally out of order if I did not mention the power of God at the forefront of your marriage. When my husband and I were first married, neither of us knew the importance of having God in our lives. I grew up in church, so I knew what it meant to go to church, but all I did was go. It was an inconsistent routine, the importance of which had yet to manifest. My husband and I both went to church together, but again; it was strictly out of routine. Then our marriage hit a rough patch. This made it glaringly noticeable that our marriage was built on sinking sand and had absolutely no foundation. We knew we loved each other, but love alone was not enough (which is a whole other story). We woke up one morning after we had argued all night, and we both agreed that we had to do something. All I can do now is thank God that we chose church as our alternative to everything else. This one move completely changed the direction of our marriage. There is nothing and no one else that I can credit except God. This one thing allowed our relationship to turn into one that strengthened, enabled us to weather storms, allowed us to be kinder to one another and more supportive of one another, and even allowed us to love each other better than we ever had before.

As women, we don't just wake up one day ready for marriage, and neither do our husbands. This is something that has to be learned. All of the things I noted above didn't just happen overnight. I can speak to those things now because I'm on the other side of those situations. Each one of those blessings came through prayer, asking God for patience, understanding, caring, and the ability to stay strong when I was weak, the ability and courage to "woman up" when need be—asking God to give me the words instead of my own that would encourage my husband, asking God to place His will for my husband in my spirit so that I could encourage him to move toward the right things (not those things that I thought were the right things). Would it be in God's plan for your husband to go out and sell drugs to provide for his family? Would it be good for you as a wife to encourage your husband to do this to support his family? No, because we all know that God would not tell you to tell your husband to go out and sell drugs. But what are some things God might tell you to say that would encourage your husband? He might tell you to encourage your husband to apply for that job as a waiter or as a gas station attendant. You might ask yourself, "Why is God telling me this? These jobs don't pay well. Why should I encourage him to do this?" These professions may not pay the most money and some people may think they are not good jobs. But what does this mean to you and your husband? It means that he is still providing for his family. He is still coming home at a decent hour and tending to his family. He is still going to church on Sunday, paying his tithes, learning about the word of God, and uplifting his family because of it. He is still involved in the church, serving and helping to uplift the kingdom of God. And lastly, he is not in jail for selling drugs and still able to be there for his wife, sons, and daughters, being the husband and father whom he was chosen to be. And truly, if you don't know how God works, let me tell you. That job that your husband takes as a waiter or as a gas station attendant may have tuition reimbursement. He may go back to school, get his education and get a job making more money than he has ever made before. You can never know how God will work. All we can do is walk in His will by faith and support our husbands even when we don't see how we'll make it. You can never know what blessings and opportunities will be on the other side of a situation. Again, all you can do is "women up" and keep it moving! Whatever your situation is, God has to direct your lives, or you won't see the good in your husband not selling drugs and instead working at a gas station.

In all that I have said, if you get nothing else, then *get this*: There is no way that your relationship will withstand the storms that life brings without God being at the forefront. This means that you both need to be in church learning and understanding the word of God. And lastly, yes, you can have a marriage without God, but I guarantee that it will not be the blessing to your life that God intended for marriage to be if He is not a part of it.

Kevin H.
Thirty-five years old
Married for eight years

Therefore shall a man leave his father and his mother, and shall cleave unto his wife: and they shall be one flesh. —Genesis 2:24

I believe before that happens you must ask God to prepare you for the change that will occur. No two people can happily come together without understanding the change that must happen. I really believe this to be true. When my wife and I decided to get married, we did not ask God, nor did we consult with Him about it. We had a day of marriage counseling from our pastor, but because we knew we loved each other, neither of us probably took his advice to heart. Our relationship really suffered for not paying attention. During the course of our engagement, we did not consult God on our plans to marry. We went to church every week but did what we wanted to during the week. That did not make for a successful engagement or marriage initially.

I lied to my wife before and during our marriage. Our marriage was almost over before it had even begun. But God revealed Himself to me and showed me that I could not make my marriage work without Him. That did not make things all better, but it did let me know I needed to make a change. I joined a church and became an active member, but I had not been changed. I still lied and made a mess of a perfect relationship. But God continued to work on me and showed me how to be a good husband. I still made mistakes, but praying to God helped me cope with the problems I had. God has always been working with me throughout our relationship.

The key to a successful marriage or relationship is to make sure God is in the center of the relationship. The love you can have for another person can fail because humans love conditionally. But God's love for us is unconditional and will endure forever. God is love; that is where the relationship should start. God's love will allow your marriage to stand until death due you part.

Arguments

I read an e-mail the other day that talked about arguments and how they should be intended to show love and not to win. I had never looked at it that way. Normally, when we are arguing, one person is mad about something and love is out the window. However, we must learn that we can be angry but that we should not allow our anger to cause us to sin. Ephesians 4:26 If we look at the argument as an opportunity to show love and use spiritual weapons to fight instead of carnal weapons, we will be able to solve issues without regretting the things that we say.

Spiritual weapons includes praying, lowering your voice, controlling your emotions. Listen actively while the other person is speaking. Try to see things from their perspective, stay calm. Allow them time to voice their thoughts and feelings without interruptions or being defensive. Carnal weapons include hitting, cursing, saying things you don't mean, nagging until you get your way. Did you know that nagging is a carnal weapon? Think about it, if you keep saying the same thing over and over until that person does what you want him or her to do is that Godly? We must learn to be bound in love. When you are bound in love only love will come out of you because that's what's in you. We must learn what love is and then practice being bound in love.

Some people like to make their point and make sure that the other person understands how angry they are which sometimes makes the situation worst. We should be meek even in a stressful situation or potential arguments. Meekness is not weakness it's power under control. Extend love when you are angry, allow them to apologize and forgive them. Resolve the issue and please don't bring it back up again after it's resolved.

Be able to disagree without going Rambo on them. Try to be understanding even when the person has made a mistake. Maybe even forgotten something that was important to you and you have reason to be angry remember that your mate is human. They are entitled to make mistakes; you will also make mistakes and will want their forgiveness. Leave the past in the past, and look to your future from your present, not from your past or from your past mistakes.

Some say that when they were dating they did not argue, but after marriage, they argued all the time. Some people argue all the time while they are dating and still choose to get married. I think they are expecting things to change after they get married, which I seriously doubt that it will. However, arguments disagreements are bound to happen whether you are newlyweds are have been married for many years.

To help decrease agreements as newlyweds, please realize your spouse is not going to become everything that he or she is going to be the night after the wedding. The bride on her wedding day is a woman starting on a journey of being a wife. The groom is starting on a journey of being a husband. Give each other time to grow and enjoy the journey together good times and bad times.

Let me break it down like this: Men, the woman who walks down the aisle on your wedding day is not a wife. She is a woman getting ready to be a wife. Women, that man who is standing at the end of the aisle sweating bullets (just kidding), smiling and looking fine in his tuxedo is not a husband. He is a man on a journey to be a husband. We cannot expect him to be almighty, knowing what you are thinking, knowing exactly what to do and how to do it. When this reality is in your spirit there will be fewer arguments, because you will understand that there is still a process you both must go through in your marriage to learn how to be the mate you need to be for each other.

A girlfriend of mine who was recently married was upset because her husband was not running the house like she thought he should have. My thought was *that he had to learn how to be a husband and that she couldn't drop everything on him when they first got married.* As a single woman and mother, I know that I can't wait for my husband to step in and lead and that every decision won't be on me. But the Holy Spirit reminded me that I cannot give everything to him. I am his helpmate. Together, we must learn our roles in the marriage and help each other. He is not my savior and I can't just lay back and watch him build our house. Proverbs 31, clearly states "that a wise woman builds her house." Look at the reality of your situation and remember how he handled his own household when you were dating. Men, were her children obedient to her and you while you were dating? If not, guess what? This will be an area of work and improvement for the entire family. Do not think just because you are married that the children will change. Ladies, don't get upset if he tells you that your children did this or that and he wants you to take care of it. More than likely, he has never had to discipline your children before, so don't expect him to feel comfortable doing it now. This also goes for men who are bringing children into the relationship.

Actually, this is something that I have not dealt with in this book at all but it is very important. I know a lot of single parents and future or current stepparents struggle with disciplining the children. Get your children under control now! Teach them to respect everyone and to be obedient to adults. This will cause less confusion in your marriage. It may take some time to develop a relationship with your mate's children, so give your mate time to build their own relationship with the children. I suggest starting on this during the courting period. How to raise children, discipline and things of that sort should be discussed before you get married. Come up with a plan of action for raising the children.

Another top area of arguments is in the area of finance. Especially, newlyweds because when single for a long time, often you're not accustom to sharing or being accountable to anyone on how you spend your money or pay your bills. (I pray that at this point, God has taught you how to be a good steward over your finances. If not, please pray about that, and you may want to get some financial counseling). As the old song goes, there is no romance without finance! This is true to a point, because when you are broke, love, intimacy, and sex are the last things on your mind. Building someone else up is definitely out of the question, because you're trying to get some money. (Mind on my money ... money on my mind.) Seriously, this is something that should be discussed and even practiced during the engagement. You may want to get a shared bank account, combining your money and balancing your checkbooks together. You may even consider combining bills and paying them out of both of your checks if possible. Credit scores and debt should be laid out on the table. You should know his or her financial situation. Some people have a lot of outstanding debt, student loans, and child support. That's not to say you can't marry this person or there won't be joy in your marriage because of debt. I am only saying you should be wise. If there is a lot of debt between the both of you, get that paid down. You may have to sacrifice having that huge dream wedding or that two-week honeymoon to Hawaii. Maybe you could hold off a year or so to get married if you must have all these things. You don't want poor finances to be the reason you and your mate can't get along or the reason for the arguments. I do not believe in this day and time that it's solely on the man to provide financially for the household. However, some couples agree that the wife will stay home and raise the children. If that is not the case women be prepared to work outside the home to help provide for your family. Remember the virtuous wife and mother, she comes into the marriage with money and the potential to make money for her household so that there is no lack! Proverbs 31

Patience

Patience is something that most people struggle with every day. It is something that you must learn to have, or you will drive yourselves crazy. Some become impatient with a particular situation when it's not happening quickly enough for them. They then decide to take matters into their own hands and buy that car or house or have sex with that person or marry that person. Whatever the difficult situation may be they often get frustrated and jump out there without God's blessing and that's when you end up in trouble. It could be financial trouble, an abusive relationship or marriage. But had they been waited and been patient for God's timing and season they could have avoided certain struggles. We have to learn patience because when we are patient God can give us the full picture which will help us avoid devastating mistakes.

Knowledge is power but having wisdom is priceless. There are things going on in the spiritual realm—pruning, growth, or knocking down some walls. God is moving people out of the way so that you can get that promotion in order to afford the new house and the new car. Other times, He is training you and your mate so that when you get together there won't be so many obstacles in the way. However, sometimes there are battles going on in the spiritual realm that are delaying God's word or promises to you and we need to continue to pray through those delays. (Read the book of Daniel to get an understanding about delay.)

For those who are still single with no potentials in sight, I want to encourage you to hold on to what you have asked God for believing that He will give it to you when the time and season is right. Don't try to fix this yourself because you think that you have had all that you can take. When you think you cannot hold on any longer and cannot wait on God any longer, when that wilderness experience has become too hot, know that God is still able and willing if you do not give up. He knows how much you can take.

I was at that point. I felt like *"Lord, if you don't send my husband today, I will die."* I was tired, frustrated, lonely, and horney, and I needed help, needed to feel like a woman. I felt like there was so much in me that needed to be released. I was ready to start building my life with my husband and daughter. I was ready to love and be loved by my husband. Please let's not even mention sex. I was sexually frustrated, and my mind was saying, *"Just call somebody and get you some.* What will it hurt? "The Spirit of the Lord was saying, to me *"wait on the Lord. I know your struggle. I know what is best for you, please wait on the Lord."*

When it seems that God has forgotten about you and the storm seems to have intensified, I dare you to trust God even more. When you are at your breaking point, begin to worship and praise God with all that is left in you, even if it's not much. I discovered that it is during those times when your blessing is right there, the enemy will intensify the warfare, because he sees what God is about to do in your life and he wants to steal it from you. But you have to stand on the word of God and be steadfast and unmovable, and when you've done all you can to stand, stand. Ephesians 6:13

Your Anointing

Questions to which I didn't know the answers:

- How does God want me to build this relationship?
- Do I have the power to release his potential in God?
- How will I know what his deepest needs are?
- How will I know how to meet his deepest needs?
- What is it about me that will draw him into me?
- What is it about me that make me different from other women whom he has dated?
- Who am I—the real me?

When God gave me the heading for this chapter, I was still single. These questions were in my mind from a book that I read, and I didn't know the answer to them. There were some very good points brought up, so I wrote them down for myself. Now, God is actually having me base this chapter off the answers to these questions. I prayed,

"Lord, I need a man to be able to answer these questions. I cannot base them off of someone else's experience. I need to know my own anointing for the man I am going to marry."

I began to pray and ask God to show me the answers to these questions. I have shared a few of the answers. I pray that by now your mind is full of questions that you need answered.

How does God want me to build this relationship?

The Lord wants me to build this relationship with a solid foundation. When we are mixing our foundations to build on, we need to add *t*rust in the Lord, *f*aithfulness, *l*ong *s*uffering, *p*atience's, *r*espect, *d*iligence, *p*erseverance, *h*onesty, endurance, *f*aith, *h*ope, *l*ove, selflessness, loyal, *o*bedience, *v*ision, enlightening, *r*enewing of my mind and spirit, *c*leanliness, *h*oliness, *k*indness, *u*nderstanding, *p*rayerful, *f*earless, *p*eace, *m*eekness, *h*elpful, empathy, *c*ompassion, and *g*enerosity. With all of my spirit and mind, I must give my best each and every day, never giving up but always striving to please God and do His will and bring glory and honor to His name.

How will I know his/her deepest needs?

The Lord will give you wisdom and understanding of these things. You will be anointed to discern the needs of your mate. As you grow, live, love together, and stay in communion with God, He will reveal these things to you about your mate. Remember that your marriage is not echoing the world system marriage. Even when you are upset with your husband or wife, show love, be kind, and compassionate. Continue to speak life into them. Do not tear them down with your words or your actions. A foolish woman tears down her house with her own hands (Proverbs 14:1) this also includes men.

We must learn to listen to our mates and study their habits. Pay attention to how they act under pressure and what they do when they're happy and all is well. What do they do to comfort themselves? My motto is the following: if I take care of you and you take care of me and we both take care of the children, then everybody is covered. Small things matter. Show appreciation one for another in the small things. Love each other because God is Love.

What is my anointing?

I have discovered that the relationship that I have been building throughout this journey of being taught how to be a wife was with God! I have been anointed since the beginning of time to build a relationship with Him and to worship and praise Him, not to be conformed to the worries of this world but to strive to do the work and the will of the Lord. I am anointed to bring the presence of God into people's lives. I am anointed to bring people to living water, which is in Christ Jesus our Lord. I have been created to minister to God's people through becoming the foundational mixture of love that I mentioned above. The Lord is saying that this is who I must become, not something I do on occasion. I must do and be this when I feel like it and when I don't feel like it. I must become love, kindness, I must be able to suffer through struggles and hard times and press my way through without giving up. I must believe that God will never leave or forsake me.

As you learn your anointing began to walk in it and the calling of God, those things that He has promised will come to pass for God is not a man, that he should lie (Numbers 23:19).

Seek God for your anointing. Know what your purpose is and what God has ordained you to do on this earth. When you know what you have been anointed to do and you begin to walk in it as unto God, I believe that anointing, that light, that glow will draw your spouse to you. When you are about our Father's business, you will begin to reap a good harvest, sow good seeds on good ground, and begin to walk in the abundant life that God has for you.

My advice is—and I do believe I am speaking through the power of the Holy Spirit—find out what God has anointed you for and then go after it with diligence, patience, and fervor. I do believe that God will open the door of opportunity for you to meet the person He has created for you since before you were in your mother's womb.

What Are You Going to Do Differently?

Today, my sister asked me, "What are you going to do differently in your next relationship?" This question was so profound to me. As I thought more about it, I realized that we all need to take self-examination and determine what we have done wrong and what we have learned from past relationships. With the things that God has taught us in mind, we must imagine ourselves applying those good things to our new relationships. You never know the next person you meet could be the one!

This section is for notes only. The question is - what are you going to do differently in this relationship? You have been walking with me through my journey of being single. My challenge for you is to write down the things that God has revealed to your spirit while reading this book and begin to apply them in your next or current relationship or marriage.

A few things that I want to do differently, lessons I've learned much later on my journey. First, stop focusing on being married so much! (I was on my own nerves). Stop sizing up every man I met to see if he fits into what I think would be a good husband for me. At some point my desire to be married became idolatry in the site of God. I know that's a strong statement but it is true. Anything, person, you think about more and desire more than God, is idolatry.

Secondly, become friends first. It's much easier to go through the challenges of life with a friend versus a stranger. Sometimes we forget about how important friendship is in a relationship. We get so emotional or life becomes so challenging that we throw friendship out the window. For those who are already married I pray that if you have put friendship on pause, that you purpose in your mind to start being your mates' friend. For those who are still dating or waiting for the special one, remember that friendship is in fact, key to a healthy relationship and marriage, and it is fun! It helps the time go by faster and helps you to enjoy the relationship. I will adventure to say that a great friendship is a prerequisite to great marriage!

Finally, if God has predestined you to share the rest of your life as a husband or a wife, take time and seek God's counsel about what you need to do differently. Ask Him to anoint you so that you can create a relationship that is pleasing and honorable to Him. Remember that you need not conform any longer to the pattern of this world, but you can be transformed by the *renewing of your mind* (italicizes is mine).Then you will be able to test and approve what God's will is—His good, pleasing, and perfect will. Romans12:2

Notes

Notes